The Limits of the Law:

Sentencing Perpetrators of Atrocious Crime

Recipient of the
Leiden Journal of International Law
Thesis Award (2011)

Ashleigh Shaheen

The Limits of the Law:
Sentencing Perpetrators of Atrocious Crime

Ashleigh Shaheen

ISBN: 978-90-5850-727-3

Published by:
Wolf Legal Publishers (WLP)
P.O. Box 31051
6503 CB Nijmegen
The Netherlands
Tel: +31 24 355 19 04
Fax: +31 84 837 67 00
E-Mail: info@wolfpublishers.nl
www.wolfpublishers.com

Acknowledgments

Voltaire once said,
"Appreciation is a wonderful thing.
It makes what is excellent in others belong to us as well."
For any excellence in my work, I am thus indebted to
Dr. Robert Heinsch, for his guidance
The Peace Palace Library staff, for their patience
Christina Badde, for her inspiration
Michelle Oliel, for her enthusiasm
Simone Fennell, for her interest
Fergal McNally, for his encouragement
and to Cindi and Albert Shaheen, for their extraordinary support.

Thank you.

*"I did not bow down to you,
I bowed down to all the suffering of humanity."*

*- Fyodor Dostoyevsky,
Crime and Punishment*

Table of Contents

List of Terms		**1**
Introduction		**3**
1.	**Obstacles to the Formation of a Universal Guideline**	**7**
1.1.	Nulla poena sin lege	7
1.2.	Judicial Discretion	10
1.3.	Indirect Enforcement	12
1.4.	Sentencing Procedure	14
1.5.	International Criminology	16
2.	**Sentencing Procedure and Practice**	**19**
2.1.	Factors in Determining the Sentence	19
	2.1.1. Gravity and Individual Circumstances	19
	2.1.2. The Underlying Crime	22
	2.1.3. Mode of Liability	22
	2.1.4. Aggravating Circumstances	23
	2.1.5. Mitigating Circumstances	25
2.2.	Sentence Length	26
3.	**Rethinking Intent**	**29**
3.1.	"Ordinary People": The Typology of Perpetrators	29
	3.1.1. Compliance, Deviance and Collectivity	30
	3.1.2. Culpability for the Crime	33
3.2.	Impact on Sentencing	35
4.	**Reevaluating the Purpose of Sentencing**	**37**
4.1.	Goals of Punishment in International Criminal Law	37
	4.1.1. Deterrence	37
	4.1.2. Expressivism	39
	4.1.3. Retribution	40
	4.1.4. Peace and Reconciliation	42
4.2.	Purposive Sentencing	43
Conclusion		**45**
Bibliography		**47**
Case Law		**53**

List of Terms

ECHR	European Convention of Human Rights
ICC	International Criminal Court
ICCPR	International Covenant on Civil and Political Rights
ICL	International Criminal Law
ICTR	International Criminal Tribunal for Rwanda
ICTY	International Criminal Tribunal for the Former Yugoslavia
JCE	Joint Criminal Enterprise
Rules	Rules of Procedure and Evidence
UDHR	Universal Declaration of Human Rights
UN	United Nations

Introduction

It is unique to the prosecution of international crimes that much attention is paid to the symbolic function of the law. While purists aim to separate judicial mechanisms from post-conflict reconstruction, there nevertheless exists an expectation that these processes will not only coexist, but also cooperate. Because the destructive effects of mass atrocity are "more than the sum" of the individual crimes, justice is likewise expected to be more than the sum of the years that perpetrators are put behind bars.

Despite this expectation, tension occurs in instances where international tribunals are perceived to have exceeded their legal role. Although such development is possible, it cannot be denied that it has at times detrimentally affected the rights of the accused. Nowhere is this more evident than when examining sentencing practices in international criminal law. While there is a wealth of writing on the importance of guidelines for victim participation, there are no such universal guidelines for sentencing those convicted of international crimes. This opacity in sentencing procedure makes it a necessary topic for examination in international criminal law.

The absence of guidelines is only recently identified as a notable omission. When the United Nations Security Council authorized the creation of the International Criminal Tribunal for the former Yugoslavia (ICTY) in 1993, it was the first international criminal court implemented in nearly 50 years. Its establishment led that of the International Criminal Tribunal for Rwanda (ICTR) in 1994, as a response to the horrific events there. At the time, however, it was hard to imagine such tribunals becoming routine. The Statutes for each, along with their Rules of Procedure and Evidence, were developed seemingly on a one-time basis, leaving the need for permanent sentencing guidelines to be perceived as unnecessary.

Unfortunately, this did not prove to be the case. Neither is it any longer a valid reason to ignore the need for a permanent penal code in international criminal law. In the 20 years since interest in the field was renewed, the establishment of the Special Panels of the Dili District Court in East Timor (2000), the Extraordinary Chambers in the Courts of Cambodia (2001) and the Special Court for Sierra Leone (2003) among others, have made it clear that international criminal tribunals will continue to be utilized. This makes a guideline ever more important, as it will facilitate the operations of future *ad hoc* courts. It has been argued that any future *ad hoc* tribunal or national court dealing with international crimes will likely follow guidelines set by the

International Criminal Court (ICC).[1] As the first permanent court, the ICC thus has a greater chance – and perhaps a greater responsibility – to develop a comprehensive penal code.

It seems ironic that in a time when many view international criminal law as imperative to creating sustainable peace, little effort has so far been expended in order to examine what is arguably the most quantifiable measure of its success. The *ad hoc* tribunals have been primarily responsible for the developing penology of international criminal law. After over a decade of prosecutions, it is time to look critically at what they have created.

We must also reconsider the purpose sentencing serves in the international judicial process. How is that purpose reflected in the number of years accorded to each criminal act? While the length of sentences is certainly a crucial element, identifying this as the reason to create a universal guideline fails to appreciate the true value of the endeavor. Instead, a guideline affords us the opportunity to reevaluate rationalized purposes behind the punishment of mass atrocity. By identifying them, sentencing can more effectively fulfill the aims of the tribunals themselves. If sentencing lacks such purpose, then against what standard are we to evaluate its success? Can international criminal law itself be successful if its punishment mechanism is not?

This paper will examine the sentencing practices of the ICTY and ICTR, comparing their normative guidelines and jurisprudence to answer the following questions:

1. Is there enough consistency in sentencing to substantiate the emergence of a guideline through jurisprudence?

2. What elements should contribute to the structure of a universal sentencing guideline?

3. What penological goals should be met through sentencing?

The answers to these questions will be discussed in the context of an emerging criminology specific to international criminal law, taking into account the difference in the mentality of perpetrators of mass atrocity at the level of planning versus the level of commission. The goals of punishment will be discussed at both of these levels, evaluating their effectiveness in aiding the justice process after mass atrocity. Sentencing procedures will also be evaluated against the core mandate of the tribunal as well as against the recognized

---

1 Harmon, M. and Gaynor, F. "Ordinary Sentences for Extraordinary Crimes." *Journal of International Criminal Justice* 5 (2007), at 711.

purposes of punishment. Is sentencing practice consistent with these goals and purposes? The answer to this question may also speak to the impact of a future sentencing guideline.

Chapter 1 of this book will aim to identify the major obstacles that now prevent consistent sentencing through a guideline. Chapter 2 will examine the normative standards and jurisprudence in the *ad hoc* tribunals and the ICC, comparatively analyzing factors that influence the length of a sentence. Chapter 3 will examine the relevance of the *mens rea* of perpetrators to achieving purposive sentencing. Chapter 4 will reevaluate the purpose of sentencing and punishment in light of the mental element of the perpetrator. The final chapter will suggest reforms that will allow sentencing to accomplish meaningful goals.

International prosecution is increasingly recognized as an imperative process for dealing with atrocious crime. Yet there can seemingly be no adequate punishment for such horrific acts. For crime that "explodes the limits of the law"[2] it thus becomes equally imperative that a guide exists to temper judicial discretion and to focus punishment in a way that will ultimately contribute to sustainable peace and justice.

---

2 Drumbl, M. *Atrocity, Punishment, and International Law.* Cambridge University Press, New York (2007), at 156.

1. Obstacles to the Formation of a Universal Guideline

Chapter 1 will introduce the obstacles to consistent sentencing and the creation of guidelines. The principal challenge for a universal guideline is to uphold the principle of legality in the face of judicial discretion, vague sentencing procedure, indirect enforcement, and a developing international criminology. These issues challenge the viability of a universal sentencing regime in international criminal law.

1.1. Nulla poena sin lege

From the outset of sentencing provisions, a sense of ambiguity is apparent. There is no statutory sentencing rubric, an absence that detracts from the legitimacy of punishment by undermining the principle of legality, or *nulla poena sin lege*.[3] This principle essentially mandates that punishment for wrongdoing must be in response to clear statements that the action was a crime.[4] It may also carry a higher burden to assure reasonable consistency and foreseeability in the application of punishment.[5] It is questionable whether international criminal tribunals have so far met this standard.

Penalties are set forth for the *ad hoc* tribunals in ICTY Article 24 and ICTR Article 23, identical but for reference to the specific States. These articles list the types of penalties that may be applied but remain brief in explication:

> "(1) The penalty imposed by the Trial Chamber shall be limited to imprisonment. In determining the terms of imprisonment, the Trial Chambers shall have recourse to the general practice regarding prison sentences in the courts of the former Yugoslavia (Rwanda).
>
> 3) In addition to imprisonment, the Trial Chambers may order the return of any property and proceeds acquired by criminal conduct, including by means of duress, to their rightful owners."[6]

---

3 Ambos, Kai. "*Nulla poena sin lege* in International Criminal Law", in R. Haveman and O. Olusanya (eds.), *Sentencing and Sanctioning in Supranational Criminal Law* (2006), 17 at 24-25.

4 Beresford, Stuart. "Unshackling the Paper Tiger." *International Criminal Law Review* 1 (2001), at 47.

5 Danner, A.M. "Constructing a Hierarchy of Crimes in International Criminal Law Sentencing." *Virginia Law Review* 87 (2001), at 433-434.

6 ICTY Article 24 and ICTR Article 23.

Article 101(A) of the Rules for the ICTY and ICTR does little to elucidate the specifics, stating only that the person may be sentenced,

> "[...] for a term up to and including the remainder of the convicted person's life."[7]

In addition to the general practice of the respective states, the Chamber must consider the "gravity and individual circumstances"[8] of the convicted person, as well as the aggravating circumstances, mitigating circumstances and the general practice regarding prison sentences.[9] Other than mitigating circumstances, which provides the single example of, "substantial cooperation with the Prosecutor [...] before or after conviction,"[10] no definitions are given for these elements.

In specifying penalties, ICC Statute Article 77 manages another improvement, indicating the terms for imprisonment as,

> "(a) Imprisonment for a specified number of years, which may not exceed a maximum of 30 years; or
>
> (b) A term of life imprisonment when justified by the extreme gravity of the crime and the individual circumstances of the convicted person."[11]

Additionally, fines and forfeiture of "proceeds, property and assets derived directly or indirectly from that crime"[12] may be ordered by the Court. The ICC makes further progress by explaining that when convicted of multiple crimes, the combined punishment pronounced must be at least the number of years of the "highest individual sentence pronounced" but shall not exceed 30 years or a life sentence.[13] However, without a specific definition of "gravity" or "individual circumstances" the maximum provided by the ICC hardly provides foreseeability in sentencing.
How much foreseeability is required for sentencing provisions to fulfill *nulla poena sin lege*? While human rights documents recognize the *nulla poena* principle, they do not seem to require precise penalties.[14] Domestic jurisdictions

---

7 ICTY and ICTR Rule101(A).
8 ICTY Article 24(2) and ICTR Article 23(2).
9 ICTY Article 24(1) and ICTR Article 23(1); ICTY and ICTR Rule 101(B).
10 ICTY and ICTR Rule 101(B)(ii).
11 ICC Statute Article 77(1)(a) and (b); ICC Rule 145(3).
12 ICC Statute Article 77(2).
13 ICC Statute Article 78(3).
14 Ambos, *supra* note 3, at 24. Notably UDHR Article 11(2), ICCPR Article 15(1)(2), and ECHR Article 7(1)(2).

usually fulfill the *nulla poena* requirement by creating minimum and maximum sentences for crimes[15], a practice that but has not been adopted by international tribunals. Though the ICC offers a maximum of a life sentence, this applies to all crimes within its jurisdiction.

Without a transparent rationale, sentencing could be perceived as an arbitrary calculation. The statutory instructions and the Rules of Procedure and Evidence (Rules) in the *ad hoc* tribunals grant what has been seminally interpreted as "unfettered discretion"[16] to the judges. Furthermore, a sentence is usually handed down in totality at the *ad hoc* courts, without specifying the number of years accorded to each crime, let alone each element of guilt or mitigation.

However, the unresolved debate about whether a "hierarchy" of crimes exists presents a practical challenge to standardizing sentencing ranges.[17] Perpetrators of genocide seem to receive longer terms of incarceration despite judicial insistence that there is no hierarchy.[18] The construction of a sentencing guideline would reasonably involve the adoption of minimum and maximum sentences for each crime, with a standard number of years reduced or added for mitigating and aggravating factors. Without agreement on whether there is a hierarchy of crimes, however, it remains difficult to agree on minimum sentences for each.

Although reference to domestic practice is meant to provide structure for conflicts such as this, jurisprudence has established that recourse to be non-binding and subject to judicial discretion. In *Tadic* it was held that there is,

> "[...]no jurisprudential or juridical basis for the assertion that the (ICTY) is bound by decisions of the courts of the former Yugoslavia."[19]

Although discarding the possibility of domestic sentencing in favor of discretion seems to further undermine the principle of legal certainty, the

---

15 US Federal Sentencing Guidelines 2010, accessible at:http://www.ussc.gov/Guidelines/2010_guidelines/index.cfm.

16 *Prosecutor v. Erdemovic*, Judgment, 29 November 1996, at 19. See also, *Prosecutor v. Kambanda*, Judgment, 4 September 1998, at 26.

17 Danner, A.M. *supra* note 5. Olusanya, O. "Do crimes against humanity deserve a higher sentence than war crimes?" *International Criminal Law Review* 4 (2004), at 431. Separate Opinion of Judge Shahabudeen, *Prosecutor v. Tadic*, Appeals Judgment, 26 January 2000.

18 Holá, B.*et al.* "International Sentencing Facts and Figures." *Journal of International Criminal Justice* 9 (2011), 415-416 and 436-437.

19 *Tadic, supra* note 17, at 21. See also *Prosecutor v. Delalic et al.*, Appeals Judgment, 20 February 2001, at 817.

ICTY has justified this deviation by explaining that the,

> "[...] *ratione materiae* jurisdiction...differs fundamentally from that of a national court (which punishes) usually ordinary crimes."[20]

Thus, while a Trial Chamber should have recourse to domestic practices, they cannot be under obligation to, "conform to that practice"[21] without risking an unfair sentence. Indeed, reference to domestic practices would make consistency between courts difficult, as sentencing in domestic jurisdictions varies greatly.[22] Recourse to national sentencing procedure is not sufficient to satisfy the *nulla poena* requirement when it precludes consistency in sentencing between tribunals.[23]

The inability to determine whether there is more value in consistency within a tribunal or overall consistency for international criminal mechanisms contributes to uncertainty in the sentencing process. The ICC, however, makes no provision for reference to domestic sentencing; a decision that could allow space for a universal guideline to emerge and be adopted by future *ad hoc* courts.

While regard for domestic differences is a compelling argument for flexibility in sentencing, its inconsistency presents too strong an obstacle to *nulla poena sin lege*. For ICL to maintain legitimacy, there must be a universal application of penalties that provides foreseeability in how punishment will be applied.

1.2. Judicial Discretion

Judicial discretion in determining sentences at the ICTY and ICTR grew out of the vague normative guidance offered by their Statutes and Rules. The result of this arrangement has been identified as a source of inconsistent sentencing patterns.[24] While the ICTY has held that consistency was "one of the fundamental elements in any rational and fair system of criminal justice"[25] it has also claimed,

> "[...] broad discretion as to which factors it may consider in sentencing and the weight to attribute to them."[26]

---

20 *Erdemovic, supra* note16, at 62.
21 *Delalic et al., supra* note 19, at 813. See also *Kambanda, supra* note 16, at 25.
22 Weinberg, I.M. and Rassi, C. "Sentencing and Incarceration in the Ad Hoc Tribunals." *Stanford Journal of International Law* 44 (2008), 2-4.
23 Ambos, *supra* note 3, at 25.
24 Holá, *supra* note 18, at 412, 415-416 and 436-437.
25 *Prosecutor v. Krnojelac*, Judgment, 15 March 2002, at 526.
26 *Prosecutor v. Jelisic*, Judgment, 5 July 2001, at 100. Also see *Prosecutor v. Dragan Nicolic*, Appeals Judgment, 4 February 2005, at 27.

Discretion does serve an important function in enabling the obligation of the Chamber, "to individualize a penalty to fit the individual circumstances of the accused and the gravity of the crime"[27] for the purpose of ensuring a fair sentence. After all, legitimacy can also be compromised by a mandate that is too inflexible to respond to the demands of locality and culture.[28] In this way, discretion is extraordinarily helpful for achieving perceived fairness or effectiveness. However,

> "[...] the judges of the Chamber cannot limit themselves to the factors mentioned in the Statute and the Rules [...] their *unfettered discretion* to evaluate the facts and attendant circumstances should enable them to take into account any other factor they deem pertinent."[29]

The emphasis on "unfettered discretion" seems to go beyond the requirement of ensuring a fair sentence and to disregard the principle of equality before the law. Most striking in regards to equality is insistence to the contrary by the ICTY Appeals Chamber in *Delalic, et al.* The Chamber claimed there that it was not bound to impose the same sentence in two cases simply because the circumstances between the two were alike.[30] What has resulted is a wide variety of judicial assertions about which factors are pertinent to the determination of a sentence and how much weight they carry. These factors will be discussed in depth in Chapter 2 but such variability undoubtedly compromises the principles of legality and equity before the law.

It is clear that judicial discretion has been critical for the ICTY and ICTR, whose decisions had to be made before international criminal law developed its own penology. While discretion may have been necessary at the inception of international criminal law for creating sentences that fit such extraordinary crimes, there is no justification for continuing a regime of uncertain punishment if strict principles can be established. The permanence of the ICC especially allows for fair and universal sentences to be handed down to perpetrators of many conflicts. As international criminal law procedure becomes more established, it is less useful to have such a broad discretionary power for judges. A universal guideline should limit discretionary sentencing in favor of objective criteria.

---

27 *Prosecutor v. Delalic et al.*, Judgment, 9 October 2001, at 717. This was reinforced in *Krnojelac*, *supra* note 25, at 507;and *Prosecutor v. Simba*, Appeals Judgment, 27 November 2007, at 336.

28 Henham, R. "Developing Contextualized Rationales for Sentencing in International Criminal Trials: A Plea for Empirical Research." *Journal of International Criminal Justice* 5 (2007), 776-778.

29 *Kambanda*, *supra* note 16, at 30 [emphasis added].

30 *Delalic et al. supra* note 19, at 757. Knoops, G.A. *Theory and Practice of International and Internationalizd Criminal Proceedings* (2005), at 274.

1.3. Indirect Enforcement

While the existence of international legal mechanisms is a step towards direct enforcement of international law, the enforcement of penalties remains very much indirect. International tribunals rely on States to fulfill the terms of any sentence handed down.[31] Because enforcement of penalties is left to States, responsibility for fulfilling the *nulla poena* principle has been argued to fall to their national jurisdictions.[32]

The ICTY, ICTR and ICC all rely on a list of states that have declared themselves willing to incarcerate convicted persons.[33] Problems arise when the sentence imposed exceeds the limit that is legally enforceable by the domestic legislation of the incarcerating state. These states have indicated that they will only incarcerate those whose sentences are within the domestic limit.[34] ICC Statute Article 80 is especially clear on this point, stating,

> "Nothing in this part affects the application by States of penalties prescribed by their national law, nor the law of States which do not provide for penalties prescribed in this part."[35]

This recalls the argument that judicial discretion should be preserved to allow judges to set sentences within the legal regime of the state responsible for incarceration. However, this subjectivity in sentencing has already been established to violate the principle of equality before the law. It may also present a substantial human rights concern if this results in only some offenders receiving lighter sentences simply because they are being incarcerated in states with lower sentencing limits.[36]

To the satisfaction of human rights standards, this conflict has been addressed in situations where a domestic court could implement a *higher* punishment than the tribunal. For example, the exclusion of the death penalty from the ICTR was contentious, as the domestic Rwandan penal code did allow for it.[37] There was concern that "lesser" perpetrators would be sent to national courts and receive the death penalty, whereas the "most culpable" would remain in international

---

31 Knoops, *supra* note 30, at 282.

32 Ambos, *supra* note 3, at 24.

33 ICTR Article 26, ICTY Article 27, ICC Statute Article 103(1).

34 Knoops, *supra* note 30, at 285.

35 ICC Statute Article 80.

36 ICCPR Article 15 reads, "Nor shall a heavier penalty be imposed than the one that was applicable at the time when the criminal offence was committed. If, subsequent to the commission of the offence, provision is made by law for the imposition of the lighter penalty, the offender shall benefit thereby."

37 Knoops, *supra* note 30, at 275.

jurisdiction and receive life imprisonment in relatively comfortable conditions. Preventing the national courts from applying the death penalty to cases related to the conflict mostly solved this problem. Future international courts must similarly find a way require that states parties or participants uphold the international sentence even in cases where it conflicts with domestic legislation.

Yet, separate from the determination of the sentence itself, pardons and early release are also subject to State enforcement and therefore differ between perpetrators. ICTY Article 28 and ICTR Article 27 state,

> "If, pursuant to the applicable law of the State in which the convicted person is imprisoned, he or she is eligible for pardon or commutation of the sentence, the State concerned shall notify the International Tribunal accordingly. The President of the International Tribunal, in consultation with the judges, shall decide the matter on the basis of the interests of justice and the general principles of law."[38]

This has a particular impact on States that do not support life imprisonment. They must notify the Tribunal when the offender is eligible for release under domestic law. The probability for early release can be taken into account through judicial discretion, presumably increasing the length of the sentence in order to ensure that the perpetrator spends an appropriate amount of time in incarceration.

This provokes a discussion of resources, however. As in the case of Charles Taylor, whose very arrest was contingent on the UK's agreement to incarcerate him in the event of a conviction[39], it is foreseeable that future *ad hoc* tribunals may need to rely on other States for the incarceration of its own perpetrators. Both the ICTY and the ICTR have established that judges can take into account the resources required to incarcerate a perpetrator during sentencing.[40] This is the motivation behind including, "substantial cooperation with the court" as a mitigating factor.[41] The ICC notably indicates that there should be an "equitable" sharing of responsibility for incarceration among these states, a nod to the significant resources required to incarcerate a person.[42] Clearly, limited resources further impede the probability of standardized sentences.

38 ICTY Article 28 and ICTR Article 27.

39 "UK pressed to jail Charles Taylor." BBC News, 9 June 2006. Accessed 13 June 2011. http://news.bbc.co.uk/2/hi/africa/5065562.stm. "UK agrees to jail Charles Taylor." Also, BBC News, 15 June 2006. Accessed 13 June 2011. http://news.bbc.co.uk/2/hi/5082664.stm.

40 Harmon and Gaynor, *supra* note 1, at 699-703.

41 *ibid*, at 690.

42 ICC Statute Article 103(3) and ICC Rule 201.

Indirect enforcement of sentences illuminates a conflict that complementarity has not eliminated for the ICC. Furthermore, funding is limited in every tribunal. If a guideline sets sentences that exceed the resources of a state, its contribution to the legitimacy of international criminal law will obviously be compromised. Creating a simultaneous system of universal enforcement is fundamental to the success of a sentencing guideline.

1.4. Sentencing Procedure

The use of a sentencing guideline requires a great deal more time than is currently spent on sentencing, which is usually pronounced at the same time as the judgment. Holding a hearing for sentencing separately from judgment is not required at either the ICC or the *ad hoc* tribunals, though it can be requested at the ICC.[43] As the ICC has not yet reached a judgment in any case, it remains to be seen whether it will be utilized. The separate hearing, however, is considered necessary by some scholars, who argue,

> "Such a procedure would allow the Defense and Prosecution to put forward detailed and comprehensive sentencing submissions on the crimes for which convictions have been entered, rather than making hypothetical submissions before the charges, if any, on which the accused will be convicted are known to the parties."[44]

Without a mandatory hearing after a regular conviction, the prosecution and defense have little opportunity to argue the points of mitigation or aggravation before the Chambers. A separate sentencing procedure would also help to rectify what has been identified as a cyclic pattern in the consideration of aggravating and mitigating factors. Other commentators have exhaustively identified instances in which an element of the crime is then counted again as an element of aggravation.[45] While the ICC has again improved this, by listing specific elements of mitigation or aggravation, these remain subject to judicial discretion. Judges could, for example, count "any motive involving discrimination"[46] as an aggravating factor in crimes against humanity, where such discrimination may already be an element of the crime.[47] In order for a guideline to be used effectively, a separate hearing must be available for arguments regarding the elements of punishment.

Furthermore, judges in the *ad hoc* courts are not required to explain how many years are assigned to each crime, nor must they elaborate on the number of

---

43 ICC Statute Article 76(2).
44 Harmon and Gaynor, *supra* note 1, at 708.
45 *ibid*, at 683.
46 ICC Rule 145(2)(b)(v).
47 ICC Statute Article 7(1)(h).

years added or detracted for mitigating and aggravating circumstances.[48] ICTY jurisprudence has determined that a sentence may be handed down in totality for multiple convictions[49], despite the requirement in ICTY and ICTR RPE 87 that,

> "(C) If the Trial Chamber finds the accused guilty on one or more of the charges contained in the indictment, it shall at the same time determine the penalty to be imposed in respect of *each finding* of guilt."[50]

However, the ICTY has established even this as being subject to judicial discretion, noting,

> "[...] the overarching goal in sentencing must be to ensure that the final or aggregate sentence reflects the totality [...] and overall culpability [...]. This can be achieved through either the imposition of one sentence in respect of all offenses or several sentences [...]. The decision [...] lies within the discretion of the Trial Chamber."[51]

Because judgments at the ICTY do not always include a breakdown of the sentence, ICTR judges have commented that,

> "[...] the practice of awarding a single sentence for the totality of an accused's conduct makes it difficult to determine the range of sentences for each specific crime."[52]

In order to ensure consistency in sentencing, it must be required by a guideline that each conviction be given a sentence, even if this is then modified for the 'totality' of the punishment. The ICC seems to agree, indicating in ICC Rules 142(2),

> "When there is more than one charge, the Trial Chamber shall decide separately on each charge."[53]

Furthermore, ICC Statute Article 78(3) states,

> "When a person has been convicted of more than one crime, the Court shall pronounce a sentence for each crime and a joint

48 Weinberg and Rassi, *supra* note 23, at 12.
49 *ibid*, at 15.
50 ICTY and ICTR Rule 87(B) and (C) [emphasis added].
51 *Prosecutor v. Delalic*, Appeals Judgment, 8 April 2003, at 430.
52 *Prosecutor v. Semanza*, Judgment, 15 May 2003, at 562.
53 ICC Rule 142(2).

> sentence specifying the total period of imprisonment."[54]

However, this still does not require a pronouncement on the number of years added or reduced for aggravating and mitigating circumstances.[55] Nor is it a guarantee that ICC sentencing will not similarly find that 'totality' sentencing is acceptable. Whether the ICC intends to provide such detail in its judgments remains to be seen but it would certainly be a welcome contribution to consistency and to the formation of a universal guideline.
As was discussed in the previous section, it would be difficult to require that a tribunal implement a separate sentencing hearing in the face of limited resources. However, such a distinction is still necessary to ensure that an appropriate punishment is determined.

1.5. International Criminology

It is also possible that an undeveloped criminology for international criminal law has resulted in the somewhat erratic sentencing practices from the ad hoc tribunals and special courts. Without a criminology specific to international law, sentencing procedure is simply adapted from domestic jurisdictions without taking into account the substantial difference in the mentality of perpetrators. This is due in part to the circumstances of mass atrocity, where the psychosocial paradigms of compliance and deviance are often inverted when collective action overwhelms a population.[56] Thus, the *mens rea* of the perpetrator and its definition of "intent" may fundamentally differ in international crimes. Without an understanding of how collective action impacts *mens rea*, punishing perpetrators of international crime lacks a clear purpose. Without a clear punitive purpose or a complete understanding of "intent", it is understandable that jurisprudence has yielded a range of sentences.

Mark Drumbl argues that when individuals act as part of a group and are motivated by factors specific to that group, their level of individual intent is compromised.[57] In contrast to domestic crime, where the perpetrator is knowingly breaking the law, during the commission of an international crime, perpetrators are usually acting in accordance with existing laws or social order. He writes,

> "...individual participation in ordinary crime deviates from generally accepted social norms in the place and time where the crime is committed, extraordinary crime has an organic and group component that makes individual participation therein not

---

54 ICC Statute Article 78(3).

55 ICC Rule 142(2), 145(1)(b), and 145(2).

56 Drumbl, *supra* note 2, at 32.

57 McCauley, Clark. Group Dynamics in Janis's Theory of Groupthink: Backward and Forward. *Organizational Behavior and Human Decision Processes* 73 (1998), at 185.

so self-evidently deviant. Participation is often a matter of obeying official authority, not transgressing it."[58]

For some, this may tread uncomfortably close to the Nuremburg defense of "superior orders" proposed, and rejected, during the International Military Tribunal at Nuremburg (IMT).[59] However, recognizing the circumstances that contributed to the actions of the perpetrator is not an argument for mitigation of their responsibility. Rather, it provides information about what punishment will be effective, and such crimes may be prevented. This requires judges to consider the effect of authority and group action on individuals who act outside of a militarized hierarchy.

The flexibility of judicial discretion has allowed judges to attempt to reconcile the collective influence with individual responsibility, for example, through the creation of Joint Criminal Enterprise (JCE). However, this is far from a systematic penological response to the mentality and motivations of an individual perpetrator. Without such a response, punishment cannot meet punitive goals, nor can it meet the aims of the tribunals themselves. Indeed, the ICTY and ICTR have recognized sentencing parameters to be structured around goals for punishment, which are supported by the founding UNSC resolutions.[60] Chapter 4 will discuss further the merit of these goals and whether they can result in purposive punishment given these criminological limitations.

This emerging international criminology suggests that general principles of law derived from national jurisdictions are not valuable sources for sentencing procedure. The impact of collectivity and the role of compliance are too distinct from domestic crimes. While international crimes are deviant from international law, most individuals do not have so elevated an understanding of international norms that they would be immune from destructive changes in domestic state. If this were true, situations of mass atrocity would never occur. Instead, for general principles of sentencing to emerge from national jurisdictions, a substantial study would have to be done on the adaptations made by domestic sentencing in "internationalized tribunals", domestic courts that prosecute international crimes.[61]

With the permanence of the ICC a reality, it is time to reexamine the adaptation of domestic criminology and penology to international criminal law. If international criminal law is to maintain its legitimacy, it must be held to a higher

58 Drumbl, *supra* note 2, at 24.

59 Nuremberg IMT: Judgment and Sentences. *American Journal of International Law* 41 (1947).

60 Knoops, *supra* note 30, at 272.

61 Ambos, *supra* note 3, at 32.

standard of consistency. The next chapter will look critically at the factors determining the sentence to identify how a guideline might be structured to achieve this.

2. Sentencing Procedure and Practice

Chapter 2 will examine the normative standards and jurisprudence of international criminal law, comparatively analyzing factors that have influenced the determination sentences. It will be shown that there is not enough consistency in the application of these factors to substantiate the emergence of a sentencing guideline from jurisprudence alone. An argument will be made for new definitions of these factors, which will indicate how a guideline might be structured around their significance.

2.1. Factors in Determining the Sentence

Although ICTY and ICTR jurisprudence has yielded a significant discretionary power to judges in determining the weight of elements in sentencing, the elements themselves are clearly stated, if not clearly defined, in ICC Rule 145, ICTY and ICTR Rule 101. Factors that determine a sentence are the gravity of the offense and the individual circumstances of the accused, the category of the crime, the underlying crime, aggravating circumstances, and mitigating circumstances. Because these elements are often conflated or inconsistently applied, a systematic assessment of their value is necessary to determine how a universal guideline should be structured.

2.1.1. Gravity and Individual Circumstances

The gravity and individual circumstances of a crime are the primary elements listed by the Statutes of the ICTY and ICTR for determining a sentence. The Chambers should,

> "[...] take into account such factors as the gravity of the offense and the individual circumstances of the convicted person."[62]

The ICC reiterates these standards, stating,

"[...] the Court shall [...] take into account such factors as the gravity of the crime and the individual circumstances of the convicted person."[63]

While these guidelines universally insist that the sentence consider the "gravity" of the offense, there is likewise a universal dearth of agreement on what constitutes the gravity of the crime. Jurisprudence confirms gravity to be

---

62 ICTY Article 24(2). See also ICTR Article 23(2).

63 ICC Statute Article 78(1) and (3).

"the primary consideration"[64] in imposing the sentence but does little to how it is measured. In *Krnojelac*, the gravity was determined to require,

> "...consideration of the particular circumstances of the case, as well as the form and degree of the participation of the accused in the crime. The nature of the actions of others for which the accused is found to be responsible is therefore relevant, but those actions are considered principally by reference to the nature of the accused's responsibility for them."[65]

However, in *Mrksic and Sljivancanin*the ICTY has also held that,

> "While consideration of the gravity of the offence involves [...] the conduct of the accused (and) consideration of the seriousness of the underlying crimes [...] the gravity of the crimes does not refer to a crime's 'objective gravity.'"[66]

In the first definition, the Court qualifies gravity as the particular circumstances of the case the form and degree of participation, and the nature of the accused's responsibility for the crime. Yet in the second case, the Chamber claims that while the conduct of the accused and underlying crimes are relevant to the gravity, these are not the entire definition.

With such a range of definitions in jurisprudence, scholars have distinguished two types gravity: *in abstracto* (a criminal law analysis of the subjective and objective elements of the crime) and *in concreto* (the harm done and culpability of the offender).[67] The harm done has been further defined as 'the particular circumstances of the case' (e.g. the scale of crime, number of victims, the extent of victims' suffering), whereas culpability is 'the form and degree of participation of the accused in the crime.'[68]

When the two definitions are analyzed in these terms, it emerges that the two Chambers agree that gravity must be more than *in abstracto*, or more than the elements of the crime charged. Gravity must involve an *in concreto* analysis of culpability and harm caused. Yet there remains a conflict in gravity *in concreto*, between an external standard of quantifiable harm and an internal standard of

---

64 *Delalic et al.*, *supra* note 27, at 731.

65 *Prosecutor v. Krnojelac*, *supra* note 25, at 522.

66 *Prosecutor v. Mrksic and Sljivancanin*, Judgment, 5 May 2009, at 375.

67 Carcano, A. "Sentencing and the Gravity of the Offense in International Criminal Law." *International and Comparative Law Quarterly* 51 (2002), at 609. See also, Danner, *supra* note 5, at 609.

68 Holá, et al. *supra* note 18, at "415. Quoting *Prosecutor v. Milutinovic et al.*, Judgment, 26 February 2009, at 1147.

the offender's culpability for that harm, demonstrated through their type of participation. Culpability and participation are more relevant to the individual circumstances, which implies an internal assessment. Whereas using 'harm' as the single criterion for gravity seems a far more adequate definition, making it an entirely external standard.

The separation of gravity from culpability seems not to be without precedent, as it was embraced in *Blagojevic and Jokic*,

> "[...] the governing criterion in sentencing is that the sentence should reflect the totality of the offender's conduct (the 'totality' principle), and that it should reflect the gravity of the offences and the culpability of the offender so that it is both just and appropriate."[69]

This is consistent with the interpretation of punishment in the Appeals Chamber for the *Nicolic* case, where it was held that punishment needed to be "proportionate to the moral blameworthiness of the offender"[70], which was separate from gravity. This upheld the Trial Chamber's determination that a sentence must,

> "[...] reflect the predominant standard of proportionality between the gravity of the offence and the degree of responsibility of the offender."[71]

Thus, the 'totality' principle is a measure of both internal and external factors to the crime, now defined as the gravity and the individual circumstances. The ICC Statute seems amenable to this interpretation, indicating that the "totality of any sentence...must reflect the culpability of the convicted person," requiring the Court to "balance all relevant factors" which are listed extensively.[72] Thus, a universal guideline must clearly indicate that gravity is not merely a repetition of the elements of the crimes themselves, as they are already heinous by definition. Assessing gravity should be limited to the scope of the harm and damage caused by the crime for which the offender has been convicted.

What, then are the factors for 'culpability' which make up the individual circumstances? As stated above, culpability is partially defined as 'the form and degree of participation of the accused in the crime.' The form and degree of

69 *Prosecutor v. Blagojevic and Jokic*, Appeals Judgment, 9 May 2007, at 339, citing *Prosecutor v. Mucic et al.*, Appeals Judgment, 8 April 2003, at 21.

70 *Prosecutor v. Dragan Nicolic*, *supra* note 26, at 21.

71 *Prosecutor v. Dragan Nicolic*, Sentencing Judgment, 18 December 2003, at 144. Confirmed by Appeals Judgment, *supra* note 26, at 21.

72 ICC Rule 145(1), pursuant to ICC Statute Article 78(1).

participation are most readily the underlying crime and mode of liability. They will therefore be discussed in the following sections.

2.1.2. The Underlying Crime

The underlying crime is the form of participation in a crime, or the act for which the offender is charged. For example, if a defendant is charged with rape as a crime against humanity, the category of crime is "crimes against humanity" but the underlying crime is "rape." Because there is so much debate on the hierarchy of crime, using the category as an indicator for the sentence is sure to bring on a uselessly politicized argument. If the category of the crime indeed increases the harm it causes, then evidence shows that this will likely result in a longer sentence due to increased gravity even if the category is not directly taken into account.[73] Similarly, the underlying crime will be utilized in an assessment of the harm done and therefore also indicates gravity. However, the category of crime does not necessarily necessitate a certain type of harm. It is the underlying crime that better reflects damage.

Both the category of the crime and the underlying crime are an external standard measuring the act itself and its effects. A universal guideline should therefore incorporate the underlying crime as part of the assessment of the harm done, creating a base sentence. The category of the crime, however, should not be considered as a separate factor.

2.1.3. Mode of Liability

The mode of liability is the extent of participation in a crime, which the ICTY Article 7(1) and ICTR Article 6(1) codify by stating,

> "[...] [a] person who planned, instigated, ordered, committed or otherwise aided and abetted in the planning, preparation or execution of a crime shall be individually criminally responsible."[74]

Likewise, a perpetrator may be charged with "superior responsibility" for a crime if they fail to prevent or punish the actions of their subordinates.[75] The ICC Statute codifies modes of liability in Article 25(3), stating that a person is responsible for a crime if that person,

> "(a) Commits such a crime, whether as an individual, jointly with another or through another person [...];

---

[73] Holá, *supra* note 18, at 416.
[74] ICTY Article 7(1) and ICTR Article 6(1).
[75] ICTY Article 7(3) and ICTR Article 6(3).

> (b) Orders, solicits or induces the commission of such a crime [...];
>
> (c) [...] aids, abets or otherwise assists in its commission or its attempted commission [...];
>
> (d) [...] contributes to the commission or attempted commission [...] by a group of persons acting with a common purpose;
>
> (e) [...] incites others to commit genocide;
> (f) Attempts to commit such a crime [...]."[76]

It is not stated overtly that the mode of liability directly influences the length of the sentence, and indeed there does seem to be a recognition that the highest indicator of individual responsibility, i.e. direct commission, may not always result in the harshest punishments. In *Erdemovic*, the offender was convicted upon a guilty plea of the murder of at least 70 victims.[77] While his direct commission was held to be an aggravating circumstance, he only received a sentence of 5 years.[78] Comparatively, in *Bisengimana*, the ICTR sentenced the offender to 15 years for aiding and abetting the deaths of over 1,000 victims.[79] In this case, the increased scope of the crime (i.e. the gravity) can certainly account for the longer sentence, but exhibits how individual responsibility can be determined by more than the form of participation. Likewise, in the *Seromba* case, the offender was sentenced to 15 years by the Trial Chamber for aiding and abetting the deaths of more than 1,500 victims.[80] This was actually increased to a life sentence upon appeal due to other factors[81] illustrating again how individual responsibility per the mode of liability is still partially divorced from the overall *culpability* of the offender, reflected by the increased or decreased lengths of the sentences.

Mode of liability, thus, must be taken in conjunction with other factors specific to the accused, what I have argued are better defined as the individual circumstances. In particular, individual circumstances are reflected in the aggravating and mitigating circumstances.

2.1.4. Aggravating Circumstances

While the Rules for the ICTY and ICTR merely indicate that Chambers "shall

76 ICC Statute Article 25(3).
77 *Prosecutor v. Erdemovic*, Judgment, 5 March 1998, at 11-15.
78 *Erdemovic*, *supra* note 77, at 23.
79 *Prosecutor v. Bisengimana*, Judgment, 13 April 2001, at 203.
80 *Prosecutor v. Seromba*, Judgment, 13 December 2006, at p. 104 (Disposition).
81 *Prosecutor v. Seromba*, Appeals Judgment, 12 March 2008, at 239.

take into account aggravating circumstances,"[82] the ICC makes a substantial effort to qualify this instruction. ICC Rule 145(2)(b) lists a number of circumstances that will aggravate a crime, including abuse of power or official capacity, the vulnerability of a victim, the particular cruelty of a crime or its scope, and discriminatory motives, among others.[83]

To some degree, this reflects what has come out of jurisprudence from the ICTY and ICTR. Aggravating factors from the *ad hoc* courts include the egregiousness of the crimes or cruelty[84] and, as seen with the mode of liability, the nature of the perpetrator's involvement, participation, or willingness.[85] The position as a superior or abuse of trust factors heavily in many cases, though the ICTY has noted that current case law,

> "[...] does not evidence a discernible pattern of the Tribunal imposing sentences on subordinates that differ greatly from those imposed on their superiors."[86]

Another significant factor is premeditation or a discriminatory motive, although,

> "When discriminatory intent is part of the requisite elements for proof of the crimes charged, it will not be considered separately as an aggravating factor in sentencing."[87]

This presents a problem in the attribution of aggravating factors, as both the ICTY and ICTR have struggled to distinguish these points from the gravity of the crime.[88] Not only do these factors overlap with the gravity of the crime, they are sometimes elements of the crime itself.[89] The lack of systematic assessment for these factors results in extremely inconsistent rationales for sentencing.

Aggravating factors have also been the breadth or scale of the crimes in terms of the harm caused or the suffering inflicted on victims and their families[90]

---

82 ICTY and ICTR Rule 101(B)(i).
83 ICC Rule 145(2)(b)(i)–(iv).
84 *Prosecutor v. Muhimana,* Judgment, 28 April 2005, 604-616: Life imprisonment should be reserved for cases of "particular zeal or sadism."
85 *Prosecutor v. Krstic,* Judgment, 2 August 2001, at 706.
86 *Krstic, ibid*, at 709.
87 *Prosecutor v. Simic,* Judgment, 17 October 2003, at 1063.
88 Henham, *supra* note 28, at 761.
89 Sloane, Robert. "Sentencing for the 'Crime of Crimes'." *Journal of International Criminal Justice* 5 (2007), at 728.
90 *Erdemovic, supra* note 16, Judgment, at 21.

and the youth of the victims, or other vulnerability.[91] As shown, however, it would improve consistency in a guideline if quantifiable harm were separately attributed to the gravity of the offense rather than to factors of aggravation.

2.1.5. Mitigating Circumstances

Similar to aggravating circumstances, the Rules for the ICTY and ICTR both require Chambers to consider mitigating circumstances in determining a sentence, including the two examples of,

> "[...] substantial cooperation with the Prosecutor by the convicted person before or after conviction."[92]

and

> "[...] acts under orders may be considered in mitigation of punishment but not responsibility."[93]

In Rule 145(2)(a), the ICC again improves through specification, stating mitigating factors to be the,

> "[...] circumstances falling short of constituting grounds for exclusion of criminal responsibility, such as substantially diminished mental capacity or duress,"

and the,

> "[...] convicted person's conduct after the act, including any efforts by the person to compensate the victims and any cooperation with the Court."[94]

Again, the ICC's mitigating factors broadly cover those that have evolved through the jurisprudence of the *ad hoc* tribunals. The ICTR has relied heavily on the ICTY's development of mitigating circumstances, which include the conduct after the act, conduct at trial, surrender, guilty plea, and genuine remorse.[95] Circumstances falling short of excluding responsibility have been the youth or advanced age of the defendant, duress, coercion, or superior orders,

---

91 *Prosecutor v. Kunarac,* Appeals Judgment, 12 June 2002, at 879.

92 ICTY and ICTR Rule 101(B)(ii).

93 ICTY Article 7(4) and ICTR Article 6(4).

94 ICC Rule 145(2)(a)(i) and (ii).

95 Ohlin, Jens David. " Towards A Unique Theory of International Criminal Sentencing." Sluiter, Goran and Vasiliev, Sergey (Eds). *International Criminal Procedure: Towards a Coherent Body of Law*. CMP Publishing Ltd (2008), at 21-25.

the vulnerability or low IQ of the defendant, the individual circumstances of the accused, their good character, indirect participation, or ameliorating conditions of detainees. Like aggravating factors, there is no set norm against which they are measured.[96] Mitigation has thus been best determined by factors having to do with the perpetrator himself, especially in light of the fact that they are not meant to mitigate guilt or gravity, merely punishment.[97]

Mitigating circumstances seem to collectively illustrate a perpetrator who is in some way conflicted about his actions or compromised in committing them. For example, the low sentence in *Erdemovic* was largely because of the mitigating circumstance of extreme duress, where his life was threatened after attempting to disobey the orders to kill his victims, and for earlier attempts to save the victims.[98] Similarly, the *Seromba* case, the Chamber accepted as a mitigating circumstance the "good character" of the offender, demonstrated by his status as a well-liked priest in his community prior to conflict. The latter, however, is perhaps an argument that would have better served as an aggravating circumstance, similar to the *Bisengimana* case, where the Chambers noted as an aggravating factor that the offender's individual circumstances of education meant that he should have been able to, "appreciate the dignity and value of human life."[99] Clearly there is more to determining the overall culpability than simply finding individual responsibility. The level of responsibility may be determined through individual circumstances other than the mode of commission, and thus influence the length of the sentence.

2.2. Sentence Length

Lacking objective criteria for determining sentence length, and in light of the insistence of the tribunals on judicial discretion for sentencing, it is difficult to identify trends in what factors influence the length of a sentence. By failing to distinguish adequately between gravity and aggravating circumstances, and factors precluding guilt from mitigating circumstances, it is almost impossible to discern what impact a particular factor has on the sentence. While the ICTR has attempted to establish general sentencing ranges, no general conclusions have been drawn about the "objective severity of individual sentences."[100] Likewise, without a consistent breakdown by Chambers as to each count or each factor of mitigation and aggravation, there is little to go on. The sentence length is therefore a limited way to evaluate determining factors without quantitative analysis of the sentences.[101] However, some patterns can be tentatively identified.

---

96 Sloane, *supra* note 89, at 729.
97 *Kambanda, supra* note 16, at 56.
98 *Erdemovic, supra* note 77, at 17.
99 *Bisengimana, supra* note 79, at 120.
100 Holá, *supra* note 18, at 416.
101 Ewald, Uwe. "'Predictably Irrational' – International Sentencing and its Discourse

It is not stated overtly that the mode of liability directly influences the length of the sentence. Indeed there does seem to be recognition, such as in *Erdemovic*, that the highest indicator of individual responsibility, i.e. direct commission, may not always result in the harshest punishments.[102] And, as illustrated by the *Seromba* and *Bisengimana* cases, the ICTY also holds that a Chamber is not *per se* bound to impose the same sentence in the one case as that imposed in another case simply because the circumstances between the two are alike.[103] Neither does it seem that Chambers recognize the highest penalties should be given to those in command or who have high responsibility for the crimes, regardless of their mode of liability. Assessing this element does allow a strong argument to be made for a stricter definition of the gravity and individual circumstances, which would help to place what impact the mode of liability is meant to have.

Analysis of current sentencing practices is frustrating, as all the elements for a guideline are already present. It is not that the courts have failed to recognize the importance of any factor. It is that each factor is left to judicial discretion with no indication of the relationship between the value of the element and the number of years. Likewise, though numerous Chambers take legality and equality into account, rationalizing each sentence subverts these individual efforts to make them systematic. The result is demonstrably inconsistent sentencing.

In order to resolve this problem, a universal guideline cannot simply assign numbers of years to each factor of mitigation or aggravation, each mode of liability or underlying charge. As established, there is too much disagreement between cases to suggest here a detailed sentencing matrix[104] as many national jurisdictions employ.[105] Without numeric values attributed to each conviction and to each factor, suggestions for numbers of years remain to be determined in another study.

However, it has been demonstrated that the sentence must reflect the 'totality' of the crime, which 'balances' the gravity and individual circumstances. By distinguishing gravity as the external factors objective to the crime (the harm caused and the underlying crime), and individual circumstances as internal factors specific to the perpetrator (the 'culpability', demonstrated through the aggravating and mitigating factors as well as mode of liability) resolves the current overlap between gravity and aggravating factors.

---

against the Backdrop of Preliminary Empirical Findings on ICTY Sentencing Practices." *International Criminal Law Review* 10 (2010), at 371.

102 *Prosecutor v. Erdemovic, supra* note 77, at 11-15.

103 *Delalic et al.,supra* note 19, at 757. *Jelisic, supra* note 26, at 96. Ambos, *supra* note 3, at 26.

104 Othman, M. *Accountability for International Humanitarian Law Violations* (2008), at 339.

105 US Federal Sentencing Guideline, *supra* note 15.

Worth consideration is basing the minimum sentences on the underlying offenses and the gravity.[106] Degree of participation should not contribute to the gravity of the offense or to the base sentence because the harm caused by the action is the same whether the mode of liability is aiding or committing the crime. The intent to cause the resulting harm is the same and achieves the same objective result. Aiding genocide that kills 100 people should result in a higher base sentence than committing genocide that kills 10 people. However, the aggravating and mitigating circumstances are appropriate to add or detract years after the base sentence is determined. If, as in *Erdemovic*, there was clear duress and demonstrable reluctance on the part of the offender to cause such harm, then a reduction of the sentence is justified. Had Erdemovic aided the crimes with enthusiasm, the sentence would have been far heavier, and rightly so. Likewise, the perpetrator that directly kills 10 may have the sentence increased because of the mode of commission.

However, the next chapter will elaborate on the mode of liability and the ways in which it is not so simple as to define commission as deserving a higher penalty than aiding or abetting. This will be done by reexamining the *mens rea* of the perpetrator and the requirements for intent and knowledge.

---

106 Holá,*supra* note 18, at 414-415.

3. Rethinking Intent

Chapter 3 will consider a connection between the *mens rea* of the perpetrator and the mode of liability for determining the sentence. To understand what punishment can accomplish, the typology of perpetrators must be placed within shifting paradigms of compliance and deviance in times of mass atrocity. In the context of collective action, a more nuanced discussion of intent and knowledge may be required for purposive sentencing.

3.1. "Ordinary People": The Typology of Perpetrators

As discussed in Chapter 1, an obstacle to the creation of sentencing guidelines is the lack of developed criminology specific to international criminal law. In particular, the social influences upon perpetrators of mass atrocity are vastly understudied, making it difficult to know what goals for their punishment are appropriate or achievable. Examining the few studies on the typology of perpetrators helps to establish a link between the crime and the rationale behind its punishment. An explanation of *why* the crime happened should influence the form of punishment, and thus the structure of a guideline.

The typology of perpetrators is the systematic classification of the role the individual played in contributing to the situation of mass atrocity. It is distinct from the mode of liability, which categorizes the role of the individual in relation to the crime for which he is charged. This distinction is imperative to understanding how, as the last chapter suggested, a perpetrator who has committed killing as an act of genocide may actually have a *mens rea* more similar to that of aiding or abetting the genocidal regime.

Alette Smeulers argues that perpetrator typology is,

"[...] a tool to enhance the understanding of the interpersonal relationships, the group dynamics and other underlying psycho-sociological mechanisms which can help us comprehend the root causes of international crimes. Such knowledge is a prerequisite to developing effective preventative measures and crucial to administering justice fairly. A typology of perpetrators can furthermore be used as a theoretical framework to attribute individual criminal responsibility and impose fair and just sentences which match the actual blameworthiness of the individual perpetrators and which do justice to their individual responsibilities within the collective."[107]

---

[107] Smeulers, Alette. "Perpetrators of International Crimes: Towards a Typology." *Supranational Criminology: Towards a Criminology of International Crimes.* Intersentia, Oxford (2008). 233-234.

This proposal is undeniably complex when analyzing mass atrocity but supports the theory that a sentence should reflect the individual circumstances of the perpetrator. In assessing culpability, it is imperative to understand that the overwhelming majority of perpetrators are not mentally ill.[108] Rather, they are "ordinary people in extraordinary circumstances"[109], whose participation in the crime may not be explicable through an ordinary understanding of intent. This does not relieve perpetrators of responsibility, but should influence the means of their punishment.

Research into the human drive behind compliance and deviance does much to illuminate the typology of perpetrators. The information can be used to examine the legal understanding of "intent" to question what it means for an individual to meet this criteria during exceptional periods where complying with state norms is committing a crime.

3.1.1. Compliance, Deviance and Collectivity

To understand why individuals participate in extraordinary crime requires an investigation into the circumstances of their surrounding at the time of commission. Criminologists classify these circumstances as state crime, organizational crime or political crime.[110] During mass atrocity, there exists a structure that transforms atrocity into the "banality of evil" through its normalization.[111] Criminality then becomes a matter of conforming to state mandates and new social norms.[112] In other words, during times of peace, complying with state law is the highest social good. But during times of mass atrocity, complying with state law is actually an international crime.

The experiments of Stanley Milgram and Philip Zimbardo famously illustrated the ease with which individuals can be manipulated into extraordinary acts when they perceive a legitimate authority to be responsible for them.[113] Milgram saw his study as proving that perpetrators feel responsibility to the authority but do

---

108 Liwerant, O. "Mass Murder: Discussing Criminological Perspectives." *Journal of International Criminal Justice* 5 (2007), at 928.

109 Smeulers, *supra* note 107, at 234.

110 Luban, D. "State Criminality and the Ambition of International Criminal Law." Isaacs, T. and Vernon, R. (eds.) *Accountability for Collective Wrongdoing* (2011), at 62-63. Watts, R. *et al.International Criminology: A Critical Introduction* (2008), at 209-211.

111 Arendt, H. *Eichmann in Jerusalem: A Report on the Banality of Evil* (1964).

112 Drumbl, *supra* note 2, at 32.

113 For information on the specific content of these experiments, see Milgram, Stanley. *Obedience to Authority: An Experimental View.* Perennial Classics, New York, New York (2004), 104-105 and 151;Zimbardo, Philip. *The power and pathology of imprisonment*(1971). Congressional Record, Serial No. 15, 1971-10-25.

not feel responsibility for their actions under the authority.[114] The perpetrator instead defines his own adequacy according to how well he has complied with given orders.[115] Thus, the fear of being perceived as deviant is the driving factor behind participation.[116] The case study of *Ordinary Men* further emphasize this point, in the specific context of mass atrocity, illustrating that even perpetrators who directly participate in genocidal killing may do so without embracing the ideology of their superiors, even if they are aware of how their actions contribute to genocidal consequences.[117] The fear of deviance alone is not enough to change the culpability of the offender, however. There should be a demonstrable relationship between the authority and the perpetrator's intent.

The *Krstić* judgment recognizes,

> "In determining the appropriate sentence, a distinction is to be made between individuals who allowed themselves to be drawn into a maelstrom of violence, even reluctantly, and those who initiated or aggravated it, and thereby more substantially contributed to the overall harm."[118]

Thus, the ICTY seems to recognize at least these two major groups of perpetrators: the masses of people who commit crimes on the ground, almost "organically,"[119] and the few who have carefully planned and the conditions for such an eruption of violence. Briefly put, perpetrators can broadly be viewed as belonging to the category of "planner" or "ground perpetrator." However, it would be a mistake to link these typologies directly to modes of liability. As has been demonstrated, a "planner" may be responsible for the commission of crimes through other individuals. Likewise, ground perpetrators are responsible for most of the direct commissions but may not be responsible for the large-scale circumstance of atrocity.

Planners have been described as the "criminal mastermind(s)", who differ from ground perpetrators because they,

> "[...] do not commit crimes of obedience; they conspire and initiate these crimes. They plan and order the crimes; they incite and inflame the masses."[120]

---

114 Milgram*supra* note 113, at 151.
115 *ibid*, at 151.
116 *ibid*, at 151. Drumbl, *supra* note 2, at 32.
117 Browning, C. *Ordinary Men: Reserve Police Battalion 101 and the Final Solution in Poland* (1992).
118 *Prosecutor v. Krstic, supra* note 85, at 711.
119 Drumbl, *supra* note 2, at 11.
120 Smeulers, *supra* note 107, at 245.

The planner is characterized as a political opportunist, who is aware that a common enemy, against whom violence can be directed, will bind the rest of the population in such a way that the mastermind is fanatically supported.[121] In other words, the planner is responsible for creating the collective influence, which is used as a tool to inspire ground perpetrators into direct commissions of crime.

In the ICC Statute, there is a hierarchy of the modes of liability, setting commission as being the highest form of responsibility, followed by ordering, and finally aiding or abetting.[122] The ICC Statute does not expressly provide for "planning" as a mode of liability, leaving open the question of whether those who fit this typology will be charged with commission "through another person" or with "ordering, soliciting or inducing" the crime. While it has been recognized in domestic courts that the former is possible, this usually requires a relationship of "tight control" between the two individuals, much as ordering and inducing require a form of a superior-subordinate relationship, usually in the context of a military structure.[123] However, this relationship may not exist so apparently in circumstances of mass atrocity. While the collective influence is pervasive, it is not an established structure.

The *ad hoc* courts and now the ICC have recognized the collective influence without reducing individual responsibility. Article 25(3)(a) and (d) of the ICC Statute include references to commission that is,

> "(a) [...] jointly with another or through another person [...];
>
> (d) [...] by a group of persons acting with a common purpose. Such contribution shall be intentional and shall either:
>
> (i) Be made with the aim of furthering the criminal activity or criminal purpose of the group; or
>
> (ii) Be made in the knowledge of the intention of the group to commit the crime;".[124]

These acknowledgments of collective action are essentially a codification of the mode of liability of joint criminal enterprise, discussed in Chapter 1 as a response to the phenomenon of collective action that had troubled the model of individual criminal responsibility. The Chamber used it as a means to imbue

---

121 *ibid*, at 244-245.

122 Werle, G. "Individual Criminal Responsibility in Article 25 ICC Statute."*Journal of International Criminal Justice* 5 (2007), at 957.

123 Werle, *supra* note 122, at 964.

124 ICC Statute Article 25(3)(a) and (d).

individual responsibility for commission of a crime that the perpetrator may not have directly acted in. It was not conversely considered how that collective action might diminish the overall culpability of the offender. It is the recognition of superior orders as a mitigating circumstance that demonstrates how judges already are aware that intent may be compromised through social influences.

The impact of the collective might mitigate an offender's culpability and therefore be considered an individual circumstance in determining the sentence. However, the collective may not influence all perpetrators in the same way. To understand how collectivity and compliance should be applied in a guideline, intent must be reexamined.

3.1.2. Culpability for the Crime

Individual criminal responsibility is the cornerstone of international criminal law, denoting that only individual people can be held accountable for their actions, not states and not amorphous "collectives."[125] However, it has been established that superior orders may be a mitigating circumstance, if not a defense to guilt. Likewise, the recognition of motive or discriminatory intent as mitigating factors also point to *mens rea* as being significant for punishment. Understanding what social influences motivated the crime is not an argument for absolving perpetrators of responsibility, as many commentators understandably fear.[126] It is a means to determine culpability so that an appropriate punishment may be formulated.

The intent and knowledge of the perpetrator form the mental element of the crime and the basis for criminal responsibility, explained in ICC Article 30:

> "(1) [...] a person shall be criminally responsible and liable for punishment [...] only if the material elements are committed with intent and knowledge.
>
> (2) [...] a person has intent where:
>
> (i) In relation to conduct, that person means to engage in the conduct;
> (ii) In relation to a consequence, that person means to cause that consequence or is aware that it will occur in the ordinary course of events."[127]

---

125 Nuremberg IMT, *supra* note 59, at 221.
126 Werle, *supra* note 122, at 953.
127 ICC Statute Article 30(1).

Fulfilling the mental element of the underlying crime automatically imbues international perpetrators with "intent" towards their actions, regardless of their mode of liability. However, the perpetrator who has planned the crimes from a position of authority has a very different "intent" than a perpetrator on the ground, who usually commits them. The principle failure of sentencing thus is not that these differing modes of participation result in individual criminal responsibility, but that it does not take into account the difference in culpability that emerges once intent is viewed as a product of the type of perpetrator. International criminal law already recognizes that those "most responsible" for committing the crimes are the ones who need to be brought to justice. However, that category has been defined rather broadly and has included both planners and ground perpetrators. While the ground perpetrator's intent toward the conduct fulfills the criteria of Article 30, it is possible that sentencing needs to distinguish between planners and ground perpetrators in determining purposive punishment.

It is clear that the rank of the offender is already recognized as an aggravating or mitigating factor, for judgments often comment that,

> "[...] the most senior members of the command structure, that is, the leaders and planners of a particular conflict, should bear heavier criminal responsibility than those lower down the scale, such as the foot soldiers carrying out the orders."[128]

However, the rank of the offender is not necessarily indicative of the level of culpability. Superior orders are recognized as a mitigating factor, reflecting the fact that at least within a military structure the influence of the superior is a paramount factor upon the actions of the subordinate. What the typology of perpetrators illustrates is that this influence exists outside the command structure of the military and pervades the general populace through the collective influence. Thus, while the tribunals have recognized the foundation for such a relationship in the context of a militarized structure and expanded responsibility through modes of participation such as JCE and command responsibility, this has not yet been considered on a broader scale of impact on the likelihood of mass atrocity occurring.

Thus, a more nuanced discussion of the intent of the perpetrator as an individual circumstance is merited at sentencing, not only in determining the influence of the superior but also in determining the influence of the collective. The direct commission of a killing, to use the earlier example, may reflect intent that is more akin to aiding and abetting crimes against humanity that were actually planned and brought about by authorities in the state. In this sense, the planning

---

128 *Prosecutor v. Musema*, Appeals Judgment, 16 November, 2001, at 383.

of the crime is a means of direct commission through masses of people who have been purposely manipulated for the task of doing so.

3.2. Impact on Sentencing

The difference in the mental element between types of perpetrators is ignored by the maladaptation of domestic sentencing practices to international crimes, discussed in Chapter 1. As a result, the punishment of international crimes currently cannot take into account the circumstances of collectivity in the crime's commission or the inversion of deviance and compliance during times of mass atrocity. Although the ICC recognizes joint commission, this is analyzed only inasmuch as it expands responsibility. It is not recognition of how collectivity drives the commission of the crime and is not used in assessing the individual circumstances of the perpetrator or his culpability.

Such evidence indicates that sentencing needs to be conducted in such a way that judges can analyze the mental element and mode of liability for circumstances where collectivity and compliance exercised a great influence over the perpetrator. Far from mitigating the gravity of the crime or the responsibility of the individual, these instances should become part of the assessment of the "individual circumstances" of the perpetrator in mitigation of punishment. By illuminating these instances, international criminal law will do much to help explain how mass atrocity occurs and perhaps how it can be prevented.

In order to determine appropriate sentences, however, the goals of punishment must first be clear, for both the tribunals and for international criminal law. Sentencing practices must reflect the mentality of the perpetrator in order to be purposive. If perpetrators with different typologies are sentenced similarly, the failure to distinguish between them will lead Chambers to attempt to achieve the same goal in each punishment. But if the ground perpetrator was acting as part of a collective, then the same goals could not be achieved as those applied to the planner.

If most "ordinary people" would act the same way under circumstances of mass atrocity, how does this change sentencing goals? The next chapter will discuss the goals of punishment and of international criminal law, evaluating how a deeper understanding of perpetrator typology is necessary for purposive sentencing.

4. Reevaluating the Purpose of Sentencing

Chapter 4 will examine the goals of punishment and discuss how they can be achieved through sentencing at international courts. It will be shown how an assessment of the individual perpetrator is necessary for sentencing that meets its own aims as well as the aims of international criminal law. Judges must look for areas of integration to give punishment greater value.

4.1. Goals of Punishment in International Criminal Law

The ICTY and ICTR have recognized sentencing parameters to be structured around the goals set forth in the founding UNSC resolutions.[129] While the most common goals stated by judges of the ICTY and ICTR are retribution and deterrence, others such as reconciliation and expressivism are being mentioned with increasing frequency. Likewise, the ICC, ICTY and ICTR share the goal of contributing to the creation of a sustainable peace by providing a mechanism of legal redress to atrocious crime that will forestall vigilante justice by promoting reconciliation. However, they also identify aims for international criminal law that can be compared to retribution, deterrence and expressivism.[130] For a sentencing guideline to achieve purposive punishment, it must be developed in light of the achievability of these goals within the individual circumstances of the perpetrator.

4.1.1. Deterrence

The function of deterrence is to prevent similar crimes from reoccurring by providing a punitive example. Deterrence is well established as a secondary focus in the ICTY although its credibility as a goal is still debated.[131] This is because it is almost impossible to prove that punishment has a deterrent effect in atrocious crime.[132]

However, it is recognized in the Rome Statute recognizes that the Court is,

---

129 Knoops, *supra* note 30, at 272.

130 While rehabilitation is the most relevant sentencing objective according to ICCPR Article 10(3), it is mentioned very infrequently in case law and therefore cannot be addressed here. It would be worthwhile in future criminological studies to consider which categories of perpetrator would benefit from rehabilitative punishment.

131 Farer, T. "Restraining the Barbarians." *Human Rights Quarterly* 22 (2000), at 93. Golash, Deirdre. "The Justification of Punishment in the International Context." *International Criminal Law and Philosophy* (2010), at 215.

132 Yet, there is evidence that legal advisors to states during wartime are curtailing the actions of military commanders and strategists to conform to IHL. Golash, *supra* note 131, at 218.

> "Determined to put an end to impunity for the perpetrators of these crimes and *thus to contribute to the prevention of such crimes...*"[133]

Any redress taken by the Court, including sentencing, is meant to contribute to creating an environment where mass atrocity is more difficult to achieve or less likely to happen. Both the ICTY and ICTR again employ similar language to emphasize deterrence, though this is not stated as a goal so clearly as by the ICC. In this case, the United Nations was,

> "Determined *to put an end to such crimes* and to take effective measures to bring to justice the persons responsible for them..."[134]

The deterrent goal is an excellent illustration of the relationship between punishment and the mode of liability or mental element. Deterrence

> "[...] seeks to operate on the will of the individual offender at the moment of temptation of commit the crime (by countering) the social pressure of the subgroup as well as the motivation of self-interest."[135]

For perpetrators who have the time and capacity to plan the large-scale commission of crime, it is far more likely that they will also have the capacity to consider the risk of international prosecution. Because deterrence operates on the perpetrator at the moment of commission, planners have a greater capacity to appreciate the threat of prosecution and subsequent punishment, especially if that punishment is laid out in something as clearly as sentencing guidelines.

However, these requirements cannot apply to nearly any participant in mass atrocity except those who qualify as planners. Perpetrators like child soldiers "are in no position" to weigh the risks and benefits of complying with their superiors or being prosecuted at an international tribunal.[136] Likewise, those caught up in waves of hatred and nationalism are usually unaware of their own responsibility[137] and thus cannot easily be motivated to consider the risk of punishment. This does not absolve them of responsibility but it shifts the form that punishment must take in order to make them aware of their responsibility.

Yet, punishment may not achieve deterrence at the international level in the

---

133 Preamble to the Rome Statute.

134 UN Doc. S/RES/808 (1993), UN Doc. S/RES/827 (2003), UN Doc. S/RES/955 (1994).

135 Golash, *supra* note 131, at 211.

136 Golash, *supra* note 131, at 211.

137 Milgram, *supra* note 113, at 150-155.

same way that it does at the domestic level. The relationship between offenders, victims and the punishing body is different. This is in part because failure to prosecute at the international level is not necessarily perceived as "condoning" the crime, the way it often is at the domestic level.[138] There is no expectation for every atrocious crime to be prosecuted in an international tribunal or court and so the selectivity of prosecution may not have any relevance to deterrence.

However, deterrence seems inherently to be linked with the ability of international tribunals to support the rule of law through punishment. Effective punishment may operate upon planners who choose not to follow through with criminal actions, or it may contribute to an environment where it is more difficult to carry out those actions. The latter is not deterrence but expressivism.

4.1.2. Expressivism

Expressivism is a goal that aims to instill public respect for the rule of law and, in the case of international tribunals, for the system of international criminal law.[139] As discussed, it often lays a foundation to support deterrent aims by exhibiting the strength of the international legal regime. Although expressivism is referred to in international jurisprudence, it is not considered at the same length as deterrence or retribution, which will be discussed in the next section.

Expressivism promotes the rule of law by illustrating the power of legal bodies to declare the "moral unacceptability" of the perpetrator's actions, expressing condemnation of the crime and encouraging the public to internalize the didactic response.[140] This is especially true because the process of the trial brings out information about the crimes and the systematic nature of how they were committed. The public revelation of this information becomes a "teaching moment" when it is accompanied by the "infliction of shame, sanction and stigma upon the antagonists."[141] This may also contribute to deterrence if it results in genuine education about the conditions that led to atrocity.

However, when an international prosecution is undertaken, offenders and their supporters may be less likely to accept punishment as being legitimate condemnation if elements of victor's justice or politicization are present. This is particularly true for perpetrators who fit the typology of planners. For example, is unlikely that a post-conflict head of state will punish its own party's members for atrocities that were similar or even identical to the ones committed

---

138 Golash, *supra* note 131, at 213.
139 Ohlin, *supra* note 95, at 387.
140 Drumbl, *supra* note 2, at 174.
141 *ibid*, at 164.

by the opposing, defeated, side. The ICTR nearly came to a standstill when the Rwandan Patriotic Front threatened to stop cooperating if the tribunal prosecuted its own members.[142] In scenarios such as this one, punishment may perpetuate violence rather than deter it. If these elements are part of the social narrative after mass atrocity, the legitimacy of sentencing and therefore its expressivist value is compromised.
Nevertheless, expressivism is emphasized by the founding documents. The ICC is,

> "Determined to put an *end to impunity* for the perpetrators of these crimes and thus to contribute to the prevention of such crimes,"

and

> "[...] resolved to *guarantee lasting respect for and the enforcement of international justice.*" [143]

Implicit in this language is a connection between enhancing the rule of law and effectively deterring future crimes through its force. Likewise, the ICTY and ICTR state expressivist aims, such as,

> "Believing that the establishment of an international tribunal for the prosecution of persons responsible for the above-mentioned violations of international humanitarian law *will contribute to ensuring that such violations are halted* and *effectively* redressed."[144]

Language that references the ability to "halt" violations and to "effectively" address them emphasizes that the rule of law will become strong enough through legal bodies for the international communities to take legitimate action in the face of mass atrocity.

4.1.3. Retribution

The aim of retribution is to exact punishment proportional to the gravity of the crime committed. It is the "dominant stated objective for punishment of atrocity perpetrators at the national and international levels"[145] and seems to speak more to the emotive need of communities to feel that perpetrators will suffer in some way for what they have done. Yet it is "rarely satisfactorily

---

142 Golash,*supra* note 131, at 202. For victor's justice and politicization, see 220-223.

143 Preamble to the Rome Statute.

144 UN Doc. S/RES/827 (2003)[emphasis added]. The ICTR differs only in that it mentions "genocide and other violations of international humanitarian law," UN Doc. S/RES/955 (1994).

145 Drumbl, *supra* note 2, at 150.

explained"[146] how retribution is accomplished by incarceration, much less how it is accomplished through the number of years handed down by the ICTY or ICTR.

In truth, retribution lacks credibility as a primary goal for punishing mass atrocity. Prosecution is visited upon on a select number of perpetrators, the length of sentences is not often any longer than it would be for a single murder in domestic jurisdictions, and the length of sentences are so variable that a message about the gravity of the crimes cannot be clearly set.[147] The evil of the atrocity is so profound that there is no punishment within the law that could be perceived as achieving a proportional response. For better or worse, mere incarceration will never create a sense of real justice after mass atrocity. After all, what punishment is enough? Is it life in prison? Is it the death penalty? Perhaps sentences should incorporate prolonged torture, broadcast daily to victims via webcam? Truly, there is no sentence that could match the magnitude of mass atrocity.

The concepts of justice need to expand past inflicting proportional pain upon the perpetrator. Granted, the "proportionality" theory is attractive to individuals on a visceral, understandable level. However, pure retribution reduces our idea of justice to the base notion of vengeance. Conflating these two concepts risks perpetuating the cycle of violence rather than leading to its resolution. In the face of mass atrocity, a proportional response should be to undo the damage, to restore order, to accomplish something for the community.

Thus, sentencing guidelines should implement "purposive retribution" as a goal of punishment, much as sentencing itself should be purposive. Retribution must be considered not as an end to itself but rather for its value in contributing to the realization of other goals of punishment and international criminal law.

Retributive aims are stated as a goal by both the *ad hoc* courts and by the ICC. The ICC by, "Affirming that (these crimes) *must not go unpunished...*"[148], and the ICTY and ICTR by stating that they are,

> "Determined to put an end to such crimes and to take effective measures *to bring to justice the persons responsible for them...*"[149]

Retribution is thus embraced as the primary definition for justice.[150] If

---

146 Harmon and Gaynor, *supra* note 1, at 692.
147 Drumbl, *supra* note 2, at 151-157.
148 Preamble to the Rome Statute.
149 UN Doc. S/RES/808 (1993), UN Doc. S/RES/827 (2003), UN Doc. S/RES/955 (1994).
150 Glickman, A. "Victim's Justice: Legitimizing the Sentencing Regime of the

facilitating sustainable peace is one goal of international criminal law, then the punishment enacted by them cannot aggravate the factors that led to the inception of the conflict. Sentencing practices that do nothing to resolve the conflict, or serve to perpetuate it further, contravene the entire purpose of international criminal law.

4.1.4. *Peace and Reconciliation*

While it is virtually unheard of to frame punishment in the language of sustainable peace, elements of this aim are very much present in sentencing. Goals stated by judges include reconciliation, restoration, reconstruction and restorative justice[151], all of which are recognize the fact that punishment plays a necessary part in creating order in post-conflict societies. It is possible that to achieve these goals, purposive retribution could serve as validation for affected communities. If public and legal retribution is exacted upon the perpetrator, the theory is that communities will be more capable of reconciling in a peaceful manner. International criminal tribunals and courts channel that anger through a legal mechanism in order to preclude vigilante justice.

This aim cannot be fully realized without a sentencing guideline that accurately accounts for the individual circumstances of perpetrators, whose actions cannot be modified nor prevented without effective punishment. Sentencing procedure remains inconsistent, violates legality, does not ensure equality before the law and is frequently perceived to be the result of victors' justice (when the sentences are too harsh), a weak tribunal (when the sentences are too light), and sometimes both. Sentencing, and thus punishment, lack legitimacy at an international level. This does nothing to end the cycles of violence that international criminal law is concerned with preventing.

The goal of sustainable peace is arguably the most significant identified by the ICC, ICTY and ICTR, as the founding instruments repeatedly recognize that mass atrocity threatens the security and stability of the international community. Such impact is of course the reason behind the response to mass atrocity being an international rather than domestic effort. The preamble to the Rome Statute is clear on this point,

> "Recognizing that such grave crimes *threaten the peace, security and well-being of the world* [...]"[152]

International Criminal Court." *Colombia Journal of Transnational Law* 43 (2005), at 229.

151 Henham, *supra* note 28, at 776.

152 Preamble to the Rome Statute [emphasis added].

The founding resolutions of the ICTY and ICTR use identical language in identifying the goal of sustainable peace,

> "Determining that this situation *constitutes a threat to international peace and security* [...]"[153]

This is followed by the assertion that the UN is,

> "[...] convinced that [...] the establishment of an international tribunal would enable this aim to be achieved and would contribute *to the restoration and the maintenance of peace* [...]"[154]

Surprisingly, reconciliation is only mentioned by the resolution for the ICTR, stating,

> "Convinced that in (Rwanda), the prosecution of persons responsible for serious violations of international humanitarian law would enable this aim to be achieved and would *contribute to the process of national reconciliation* and to the restoration and maintenance of peace [...]"[155]

In tribunals such as Rwanda, created for single localities, identifying reconciliation as a necessary aspect of sustainable peace is appropriate. However, it is unsurprising that the ICC would not identify such a goal, as it is not a supranational body and to engage in national reconciliation would perhaps be infringing on the rights of states. Perhaps ICC judges should not aim to consider what sentence might contribute to national reconciliation as many of the obstacles referenced in Chapter 1, particularly the conflict of cultural views on punishment and judicial discretion, would be difficult to overcome.

4.2. Purposive Sentencing

Incarceration and sentencing practices currently fail to achieve their goals in punishment, particularly those of deterrence and retribution. It is clear that

---

153 UN Doc. S/RES/808 [emphasis added]. This is reiterated by UN Doc. S/RES/827 (2003), UN Doc. S/RES/1166 (1998)and UN Doc. S/RES/1329 (2000). The only difference in the language of the ICTR is, "[...] this situation *continues to constitute* a threat to international peace and security [...]" UN Doc. S/RES/955 (1994) [emphasis added].

154 UN Doc. S/RES/808, reiterated by UN Doc. S/RES/827 (2003)[emphasis added]. The ICTR language is identical, except that it identifies "violations of international humanitarian law" specifically. UN Doc. S/RES/955 (1994), reiterated by UN Doc. S/RES/1165 (1998).

155 UN Doc. S/RES/955 (1994), reiterated by UN Doc. S/RES/1165 (1998).

these goals are too limited in the context of mass atrocity, and that international criminal law must be considered insufficient in itself to accomplish them. For international tribunals to meet their goal of sustainable peace, sentencing must be more systematically guided by those same goals. If punishment fails to support the structure of international criminal law, the latter may eventually be undermined.

Utilizing the typology of the perpetrator and differentiating between their intents and culpability allows judges to look at the totality of a crime within the conflict and create a sentence that upholds the goals of the tribunal. While there is ultimately debate in the arguments for which goals are most achievable in sentencing, this is perhaps because commentators are not referencing the same typology and therefore cannot account for how punishment will enact change upon the mentality of those who commit atrocious crime. What is agreed, however, is that punishment's success depends very much on the perpetrator's individual circumstances. Thus, in analyzing the mode of liability and the perpetrator's intent, judges must take care to distinguish between the culpability of perpetrators. Although they each ultimately bear individual responsibility, punishing planners with life sentences will do much to contribute to deterrence. Punishing ground perpetrators with life sentences may seem to meet retributive goals, but may ultimately further a cycle of violence. Punishment of this group has a stronger benefit in expressivism and reconciliation, if the sentences are proportional to the culpability.

If sentencing presents the international community with a "teaching moment", where culpability and goals can be explained and rationalized, then a consistent guideline that ensures equality before the law is the strongest argument against those who claim that punishment is an overly-political process. Sentencing can overcome this threat to the goals of international criminal law by specifying an analysis of the mode of liability and mental element in determining appropriate punishment. Sentencing also becomes best opportunity for the international community to disseminate information about the circumstances that contribute to mass atrocity. By doing so, international criminal law has the opportunity to educate individuals about the influence of authority and collectivity, making it more likely that the deterrence will affect ground perpetrators in the periods preceding violence. Meeting deterrent and expressivist aims thus hinges on the ability to educate individuals about their own behavior during conflict. The difference between retributive and purposive punishment may thus be the difference between mass atrocity and sustainable peace.

Conclusion

This book has examined the process of sentencing perpetrators of mass atrocity, arguing that the punishment mechanism must be applied with greater consistency and richer rationalization. The disparity between the judges' purported theory behind punishment and the sentences rendered serves to illustrate the importance of developing a universal guideline for sentencing.

It has also identified elements that should be incorporated into the creation of such a guideline. For consistent and transparent sentencing, mandatory separate hearings should be held, the definitions of gravity and individual circumstances should be clarified, individualized goals should be selected, and universal enforcement mechanisms should be in place.

The totality of the crime should be measured through the gravity and individual circumstances of the perpetrator, where gravity is the underlying crime and harm done. Individual circumstances should then be the aggravating and mitigating factors inasmuch as they reflect the true culpability of the offender, through indicators such as "intent as a planner" or the mode of liability. The base sentence should possible be determined through setting minimum sentences for the underlying offenses and then incorporating the gravity of the individual crime.[156] Individual circumstances should then add or detract from the base sentence, reflecting the total culpability. A particular indicator of culpability should be the influence of compliance or collective action, demonstrating the effectiveness of punishment on the particular goals of international criminal law.

Examination of the typology of perpetrators reveals that the role of the perpetrator, distinguishing in particular between those in roles of planning versus roles of ground perpetration, needs to be systematically accounted for in a guideline to determine which goal to apply. Doing so would ensure that appropriate punishment is meted out according to the mentality and culpability of a specific perpetrator. While retribution is now the foremost aim of punishment, it may lack credibility. It seems to fall short of its own aims, even serving to perpetuate conflict in cases where politicization and victor's justice are perceived to be influencing the justice process. To achieve purposive punishment, deterrence, expressivism, and sustainable peace are all more legitimate goals for a guideline to incorporate. By doing so, the punishment can contribute to the minimization of mass atrocity by helping to discover the means by which it is achieved.

---

156 Holá, *et al.*, *supra* note 20, at 414-415.

A sentencing regime for international criminal law presents the opportunity to increase the legitimacy of international punishment and to deter mass atrocity by promoting the international rule of law. Achieving these goals through punishment, however, requires a greater understanding of why individuals are willing to commit such extraordinary acts. Responsibility for atrocious crime is uniquely held by the individual. Punishment for such crimes should be unique to them as well.

Bibliography

Books

Arendt, H. *Eichmann in Jerusalem: A Report on the Banality of Evil* (1964).

Bassiouni, M. Cherif. *International Criminal Law (3rd Ed.): Volume III International Enforcement.* Martinus Nijhoff Publishers, (Koninklijke Brill) Leiden (2008).

Browning, Christopher R. *Ordinary Men: Reserve Battalion 101 and the Final Solution in Poland.* Harper Perennial, New York (1998).

Chehtman, Alejandro. *The Philosophical Foundations of Extraterritorial Punishment.* Oxford University Press, Oxford (2010).

Cryer, Robert, *et al. An Introduction to International Criminal Law and Procedure.* Cambridge University Press, Cambridge (2007).

Drumbl, Mark. *Atrocity, Punishment, and International Law.* Cambridge University Press, New York (2007).

Ferdinandusse, Ward N. *Direct Application of International Criminal Law in National Courts.* TMC Asser Press, The Hague (2006).

Findlay, Mark and Henham, Ralph. *Beyond Punishment: Achieving International Criminal Justice.* Palgrave Macmillan, New York (2010).

Haveman, Roelof and Olusanya, Olaoluwa (eds). *Sentencing and Sanctioning in Supranational Criminal Law.* Intersentia, Antwerp-Oxford (2006).

Henham, Ralph. *Punishment and Process in International Criminal Trials.* Ashgate Publishing Limited, Hants (2005).

Isaacs, Tracy and Vernon, Richard (eds). *Accountability for Collective Wrongdoing.* Cambridge University Press, Cambridge (2011).

Knoops, Geert-Jan Alexander. *Theory and Practice of International and Internationalizd Criminal Proceedings* (2005).

Milgram, Stanley. *Obedience to Authority: An Experimental View.* Perennial Classics, New York, New York (2004).

Olusanya, Olaoluwa. *Sentencing War Crimes and Crimes against Humanity under the International Criminal Tribunal for the Former Yugoslavia.* Europa Law Publishing, Groningen (2005).

Othman, Mohamed C. *Accountability for International Humanitarian Law Violations: The Case of Rwanda and East Timor.*

Shoham, Shlomo Giora, et al. (eds). *International Handbook of Penology and Criminal Justice.* CRC Press, Boca Raton (2008).

Taulbee, James Larry. *International Crime and Punishment.* Praeger Security International, ABC-CLIO, LLC, Santa Barbara (2009).

Watts, Rob, *et al. International Criminology: A Critical Introduction.* Routledge, Abingdon (2008).

Chapters and Articles

Ambos, Kai. "*Nulla poena sin lege* in International Criminal Law." Haveman, Roleof and Olusanya, Olaoluwa (eds.), *Sentencing and Sanctioning in Supranational Criminal Law* (2006), 17.

Anderson, Kenneth. "The Rise of International Criminal Law: Intended and Unintended Consequences." *The European Journal of International Law* 20 (2009) 2, 331.

Bagaric, Mirko and Morss, John. "International Sentencing Law: In Search of a Justification and Coherent Framework." *International Criminal Law Review* 6 (2006), 191.

Beresford, Stuart. "Unshackling the paper tiger – the sentencing practices of the ad hoc international criminal tribunals for the former Yugoslavia and Rwanda." *International Criminal Law Review* 1 (2001), 33.

Boas, Gideon. "Developments in the Law of Procedure and Evidence at the International Criminal Tribunal for the Former Yugoslavia and the International Criminal Court." *Criminal Law Forum* 12 (2001), 167.

Bohlander, Michael. "Prosecutor v. Dusko Tadic: Waiting to Exhale." *Criminal Law Forum* 11 (2000), 217.

Carcano, Andrea. "Sentencing and the Gravity of the Offence in International Criminal Law." *International and Comparative Law Quarterly* 51 (2002), 583.

Cherkassky, Lisa. "What Distinguishes the Evil of Genocide and How Should We Respond to It?" *International Journal of Punishment and Sentencing* 4 (2008) 3, 110.

Clark, Janine. "Plea Bargaining at the ICTY: Guilty Pleas and Reconciliation." *European Journal of International Law* 20 (2009) 2, 415.

Clark, Jennifer. "Zero to Life: Sentencing Appeals at the International Criminal Tribunals for the Former Yugoslavia and Rwanda." *Georgetown Law Review* 96 (2008), 1685.

Combs, Nancy. "Prosecutor v. Plavsic. Case No. IT-00-39&40/1-S." *The American Journal of International Law* 97 (2003) 4, 929.

Dana, Shahram. "Revisiting the Blaskic Sentence: Some Reflections on the Sentencing Jurisprudence of the ICTY." *International Criminal Law Review* 4 (2004), 321.

Danner, Allison Marston. "Constructing a Hierarchy of Crimes in International Criminal Law Sentencing." *Virginia Law Review* 87 (2001) 3, 2001.

Drumbl, Mark and Henham, Ralph. "Plea Bargaining at the International Criminal Tribunal for the Former Yugoslavia." *Criminal Law Forum* 16 (2005), 49.

Drumbl, Mark. "Punishment, Postgenocide: From Guilt to Shame to Civis in Rwanda." *New York University Law Review* 75 (2000), 1221.

Ewald, Uwe. "'Predictably Irrational' – International Sentencing and its Discourse against the Backdrop of Preliminary Empirical Findings on ICTY Sentencing Practices." *International Criminal Law Review* 10 (2010), 365.

Farer, Tom. "Restraining the Barbarians: Can International Criminal Law Help?" *Human Rights Quarterly* 22 (2000), 90.

Glickman, Steven. "Victims' Justice: Legitimizing the Sentencing Regime of the International Criminal Court." *Columbia Journal of Transnational Law* 43 (2005), 229.

Golash, Deirdre. "The Justification of Punishment in the International Context." *International Criminal Law and Philosophy* (2010), at 201.

Grong, Hans. "A Personal Affair: Moral Obligation and the New Common Law of Sentencing." *International Journal of Punishment and Sentencing* 5 (2009), 74.

Harmon, Mark and Gaynor, Fergal. "Ordinary Sentences for Extraordinary Crimes." *Journal of International Criminal Justice* 5 (2007), 683.

Henham, Ralph. "Developing Contextualized Rationales for Sentencing in International Criminal Trials: A Plea for Empirical Research." *Journal of International Criminal Justice* 5 (2007), 757.

Henham, Ralph. "International Sentencing in the Context of Collective Violence." *International Criminal Law Review* 7 (2007), 449.

Henham, Ralph. "The Philosophical Foundations of International Sentencing." *Journal of International Criminal Justice* 1 (2003) 1, 64.

Henham, Ralph. "Plea Bargaining and the Legitimacy of International Trial Justice: Some Observations on the Dragan Nikolic Sentencing Judgment of the ICTY." *International Criminal Law Review* 5 (2005), 601.

Henham, Ralph. "Punishment and the Role of the Prosecutor in International Criminal Trials." *Criminal Law Forum* 19 (2008), 395.

Henham, Ralph. "Some Issues for Sentencing in the International Criminal Court." *International and Comparative Law Quarterly* 52 (2003), 81.

Henham, Ralph. "Towards Restorative Sentencing in International Criminal Trials." *International Criminal Law Review* 9 (2009), 809.

Hill, Frank D. "Restorative Justice: Sketching a New Legal Discourse." *International Journal of Punishment and Sentencing*. 4 (2008) 2, 51.

Holá, B. *et al.* "International Sentencing Facts and Figures." *Journal of International Criminal Justice* 9 (2011), 411.

Hole, Adrian. "The Sentencing Provisions of the International Criminal Court." *International Journal of Punishment and Sentencing* 1 (2005) 1, 37.

Keller, Andrew. "Punishment for Violations of International Criminal Law: An Analysis of Sentencing at the ICTY and ICTR." *International and Comparative Law Review* 12 (2002), 53.

Liwerant, O. Sara. "Mass Murder: Discussing Criminological Perspectives." *Journal of International Criminal Justice* 5 (2007), 917.

Luban, D. "State Criminality and the Ambition of International Criminal Law." Isaacs, T. and Vernon, R. (eds.) *Accountability for Collective Wrongdoing* (2011).

May, Larry. "Collective Punishment and Mass Confinement" Isaacs, Tracy and Vernon, Richard (eds). *Accountability for Collective Wrongdoing*. Cambridge University Press, Cambridge (2011), at 169.

McCauley, Clark. Group Dynamics in Janis's Theory of Groupthink: Backward and Forward. *Organizational Behavior and Human Decision Processes* 73 (1998), at 185.

Meernik, James and King, Kimi. "The Sentencing Determinants of the International Criminal Tribunal for the Former Yugoslavia: An Empirical and Doctrinal Analysis." *Leiden Journal of International Law* 16 (2003), 717.

Mullins, Christopher. "The Ability of the International Criminal Court to Deter Violations of International Criminal Law: A Theoretical Assessment." *International Criminal Law Review* 10 (2010), 771.

Nemitz, Jan Christoph. "The Law of Sentencing in International Criminal Law: The Purposes of Sentencing and the Applicable Method for the Determination of the Sentence." *Yearbook of International Humanitarian Law* 4 (2001), 87.

Nemitz, Jan Christoph. "Sentencing and Punishment." *Criminal Law Forum* 18 (2007), 395.

Ntanda Nsereko, Daniel. "The Role of the International Criminal Tribunals in the Promotion of Peace and Justice: The Case of the International Criminal Court." *Criminal Law Forum* 19 (2008), 373.

Nuremberg IMT: Judgment and Sentences. *American Journal of International Law* 41 (1947).

Ohlin, Jens David. " Towards A Unique Theory of International Criminal Sentencing." Sluiter, Goran and Vasiliev, Sergey (Eds). *International Criminal Procedure: Towards a Coherent Body of Law*. CMP Publishing Ltd (2008), 381.

Olusanya, Olaoluwa. "Do crimes against humanity deserve a higher sentence than war crimes?" *International Criminal Law Review* 4 (2004), 431.

Penrose, Mary Margaret. "Lest We Fail: The Importance of Enforcement in International Criminal Law." *American University International Law Review* 15 (2000), 321.

Schabas, William. "Sentencing by International Tribunals: A Human Rights Approach." *Duke Journal of Comparative and International Law* 7 (1997), 461.

Schabas, William. "War Crimes, Crimes Against Humanity and the Death Penalty." *Albany Law Review* 60 (1996), 733.

Sloane, Robert. "Sentencing for the 'Crime of Crimes'." *Journal of International Criminal Justice* 5 (2007), 713.

Smeulers, Alette, *et al.* "Is ICTY Sentencing Predictable? An Empirical Analysis of ICTY Sentencing Practice." *Leiden Journal of International Law* 22 (2009), 79.

Smeulers, Alette. "Perpetrators of International Crimes: Towards a Typology." *Supranational Criminology: Towards a Criminology of International Crimes.* Intersentia, Oxford (2008).

Starygin, Stan. "Judicial Discretion in ECCC Decisions on Pre-trial Detention against the Backdrop of the Case-law of the International Criminal Tribunals." *International Criminal Law Review* 11 (2011), 315.

Tallgren, Immi. "The Sensibility and Sense of International Criminal Law." *European Journal of International Law* 13 (2002), 561.
Tracol, Xavier. "The Appeals Chambers of the International Criminal Tribunals." *Criminal Law Forum* (2001) 12, 137.
Van Der Merwe, Annette. "Minimum Sentences in Child Sexual Abuse Cases: The After-Effects of Rape as a Factor in Imposing Life Imprisonment." *Criminal Law Forum* 15 (2004), 301.
Van Zyl Smit, Dirk and Ashworth, Andrew. "Disproportionate Sentences as Human Rights Violations." *The Modern Law Review* 67 (2004) 4, 541.
Van Zyl Smit, Dirk. "International Imprisonment." *International and Comparative Law Quarterly* 54 (2005), 357.
Vernon, Richard. "Punishing Collectives: States or Nations?" Isaacs, Tracy and Vernon, Richard (eds). *Accountability for Collective Wrongdoing*. Cambridge University Press, Cambridge (2011), at 287.
Vrdoljak, Ana. "Genocide and Restitution: Ensuring Each Group's Contribution to Humanity." *European Journal of International Law* 22 (2011) 1, 17.
Wandall, Rasmus. "Equality by Numbers or Words: A Comparative Study of Sentencing Structures in Minnesota and in Denmark." *Criminal Law Forum* 17 (2006), 1.
Warner, Kate. "Mandatory Sentencing and the Role of the Academic." *Criminal Law Forum* 18 (2007), 321.
Weinberg de Roca, Ines Monica and Rassi, Christopher. "Sentencing and Incarceration in the Ad Hoc Tribunals." *Stanford Journal of International Law* 1 (2008), 44.
Werle, Gerhard. "Individual Criminal Responsibility in Article 25 ICC Statute." *Journal of International Criminal Justice* 5 (2007), 953.
Williams, Sarah. "ICTY Referrals to National Jurisdictions: A Fair Trial or a Fair Price?" *Criminal Law Forum* 17 (2006), 177.
Zimbardo, Philip. *The power and pathology of imprisonment* (1971). Congressional Record, Serial No. 15, 1971-10-25. Hearings before Subcommittee No. 3, of the Committee on the Judiciary, House of Representatives, Ninety-Second Congress, *First Session on Corrections, Part II, Prisons, Prison Reform and Prisoner's Rights: California*. Washington, DC: U.S. Government Printing Office.

Case Law

ICTY

Prosecutor v. Blagojevic and Jokic, IT-02-60, Appeals Judgment, 9 May 2007.

Prosecutor v. Blaskic, IT-95-14, Appeals Judgment, 29 July 2004.

Prosecutor v. Delalic et al., IT-96-21-A, Appeals Judgment, 20 February 2001.

Prosecutor v. Delalic et al., IT-96-21-T*bis*-R117, Judgment, 9 October 2001.

Prosecutor v. Delalic et al., IT-96-21-A*bis*, Appeals Judgment, 8 April 2003.

Prosecutor v. Erdemovic, IT-96-22-T1, Judgment, 29 November 1996.

Prosecutor v. Erdemovic, IT-96-22, Judgment, 5 March 1998.

Prosecutor v. Furundzija, IT-95-17/1-T, Judgment, 10 December 1998.

Prosecutor v. Jelisic, IT-95-10, Judgment, 14 December 1999.

Prosecutor v. Jelisic, IT-95-10, Appeals Judgment, 5 July 2001.

Prosecutor v. Krnojelac, IT-97-25, Judgment, 15 March 2002.

Prosecutor v. Kunarac et al., IT-96-23, Appeals Judgment, 12 June 2002.

Prosecutor v. Krstic, IT-98-33, Judgment, 2 August 2001.

Prosecutor v. Krstic, IT-98-33, Appeals Judgment, 19 April 2004.

Prosecutor v. Milutinovic et al., IT-05-87, Judgment, 26 February 2009.

Prosecutor v. Mrksic and Sljivancanin, IT-95-13/1-A, Judgment, 5 May 2009.

Prosecutor v. Mucic et al., IT-96-21, Appeals Judgment, 20 February 2001.

Prosecutor v. Dragan Nicolic, IT-94-2, Appeals Judgment, 4 February 2005.

Prosecutor v. Dragan Nicolic, IT-94-2, Judgment, 18 December 2003.

Prosecutor v. Obrenovic, IT-02-60/2, Judgment, 10 December 2003.

Prosecutor v. Rajic, IT-95-12, Judgment, 8 May 2006.

Prosecutor v. Simic et al., IT-95-9, Judgment, 17 October 2003.

Prosecutor v. Stakic, IT-97-24, Judgment, 31 July 2003.

Prosecutor v. Dusko Tadic, IT-94-1, Appeals Judgment, 26 January 2000.

Separate Opinion of Judge Shahabudeen, *Prosecutor v. Tadic,* IT-94-1 and IT-94 *Abis*, Appeals Judgment, 26 January 2000.

Prosecutor v. Vasiljevic, IT-98-32, Appeals Judgment, 25 February 2004.

ICTR

Prosecutor v. Bisengimana, ICTR-00-60, Judgment, 13 April 2001.

Prosecutor v. Kambanda, ICTR-97-3, Judgment, 4 September 1998.

Prosecutor v. Kamuhanda, ICTR-99-54, Judgment, 22 January 2004.

Prosecutor v. Kayishema and Ruzindana, ICTR-95-1, Judgment, 21 May 1999.

Prosecutor v. Muhimana, ICTR-95-1B, Judgment, 28 April 2005.

Prosecutor v. Musema, ICTR-96-13, Appeals Judgment, 16 November 2001.

Prosecutor v. Nahimana, ICTR-96-11, Judgment, 3 December 2003.

Prosecutor v. Ntagerura, ICTR-96-10-A, Judgment, 1 September 2009.

Prosecutor v. Ruggiu, ICTR-97-32-O, Judgment, 1 June 2000.

Prosecutor v. Rutaganda, ICTR-96-3, Judgment, 6 December 1999.

Prosecutor v. Simba, ICTR-01-76, Appeals Judgment, 27 November 2007.

Prosecutor v. Semanza, ICTR-97-20, Judgment, 15 May 2003.

Prosecutor v. Seromba, ICTR-2001-66, Judgment, 13 December 2006.

Prosecutor v. Seromba, ICTR-2001-66, Appeals Judgment, 12 March 2008.

Prosecutor v. Serushago, ICTR-98-39, Judgment, 5 February 1999.

Court Documents

International Criminal Court Rules of Procedure and Evidence, UN Doc PCNICC/2000/1/Add.1 (2000).

Rome Statute of the International Criminal Court, 2187 UNTS 3. Adopted 17 July 1998 and entered into force 1 July 2002.

Rules of Procedure and Evidence of the International Criminal Tribunal for the Former Yugoslavia, UN Doc. IT/32 (1994).

Rules of Procedure and Evidence of the International Criminal Tribunal of Rwanda, UN Doc. IT/53 (1995).

Statute of the International Tribunal for the Prosecution of Persons Responsible for Serious Violations of International Humanitarian Law Committed in the Territory of the former Yugoslavia since 1991, UN Doc. S/RES/827 (1993).

Statute of the International Tribunal for Rwanda, UN Doc. S/RES/955 (1994).

United Nations Security Council Resolutions on the International Tribunal for Rwanda: UN Doc. S/RES/1329 (2000), UN Doc. S/RES/812 (1994).

United Nations Security Council Resolutions on the International Tribunal for the Former Yugoslavia: UN Doc. S/RES/808 (1993), UN Doc. S/RES/1165 (1998), UN Doc. S/RES/1166 (1998), UN Doc. S/RES/1329 (2000).

International Conventions

European Convention for the Protection of Human Rights and Fundamental Freedoms, CETS No. 005. Signed 4 November 1950 and entered into force 3 September 1053.

International Covenant on Civil and Political Rights, UN Doc. A/RES/2200A (XXI). Adopted 16 December 1966 and entered into force 23 March 1976.

Universal Declaration of Human Rights, UN Doc. A/RES/217A (III). Entered into force 10 December 1948.

Other

US Federal Sentencing Guidelines Manual (2010), United States Sentencing Commission. http://www.ussc.gov/Guidelines/2010_guidelines/index.cfm.

"UK pressed to jail Charles Taylor." BBC News, 9 June 2006. Accessed 13 June 2011. http://news.bbc.co.uk/2/hi/africa/5065562.stm.

"UK agrees to jail Charles Taylor." BBC News, 15 June 2006. Accessed 13 June 2011. http://news.bbc.co.uk/2/hi/5082664.stm.